Make Your Photography Pay

Make Your Photography Pay

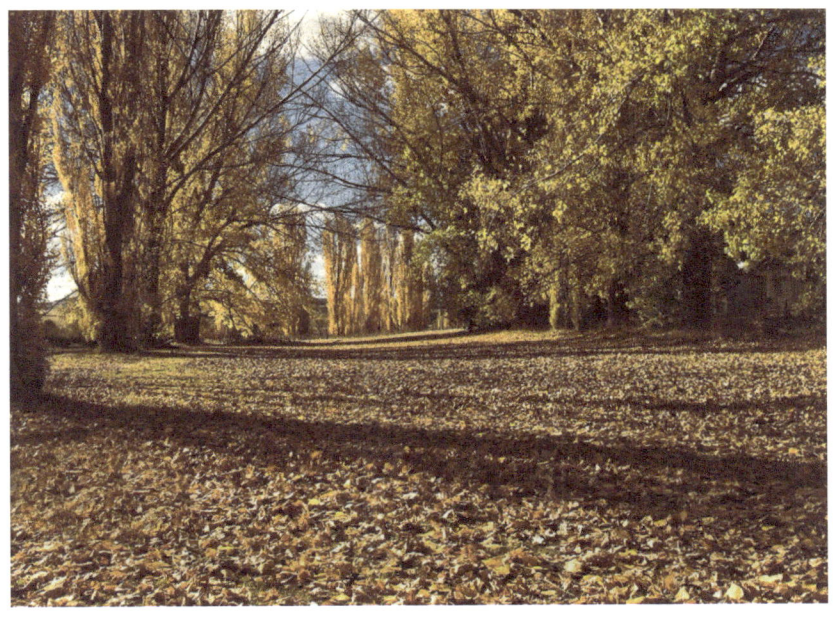

David Bigwood, LRPS

former columnist on freelancing for
F2 Freelance+Digital magazine (UK)

About the Author

David Bigwood is a regularly published writer and photographer with his work having been used in well over sixty publications.

He has qualified as a Licentiate of the Royal Photographic Society and is a member of the Australian Society of Authors.

For three years he was a columnist on freelancing for the UK magazine *F2 Freelance and Digital*. He has written regularly for *Australian Photography* and has written occasionally for *Australian Camera* and *Better Photography*.

He founded and edited *The Black and White Enthusiast* (later *Silvershotz*) and was one time editor of the *Journal of the Australian Photographic Society*.

He sells his images directly, especially with his articles, and through Alamy, the on-line photography library.

Table of Contents

NB: This book is an edited compilation of some of my e-books on Individual topics including *Starting Freelance Photography*, *How to Make Souvenirs Using Your Pictures*, and *Put Words with Your Pictures*. There are also a number of pictures from *Images that Sell*.

Introduction

Whether you want to make your photography a full-time occupation or just want to sell a few pictures to cover some of the constant expenses that photography incurs, let's be absolutely clear on one thing, freelance stock photography is a business and needs to be treated as such.

Having said that, just how realistic is it that you can make your photography pay?

I will not insult your intelligence by suggesting that there are thousands of editors out there just waiting for your contributions and willing to pay you a fortune. But, I will say that how you succeed depends very much on just how you approach the marketing of your images. A haphazard approach is likely to produce a haphazard result while a concentrated, businesslike approach is likely to bring a happy outcome.

That is, of course, assuming that you can produce quality pictures that are well composed, correctly exposed, sharp where they are supposed to be and the sort of pictures for which the buyer is looking.

Photography has never been the cheapest of hobbies and at times it seems that it swallows cash like a baleen whale gulps down krill.

So, when many years ago I found a book by Louis Peek, one of the leading freelance photographers of the day, called *Cash from your Camera*, I pounced upon it.

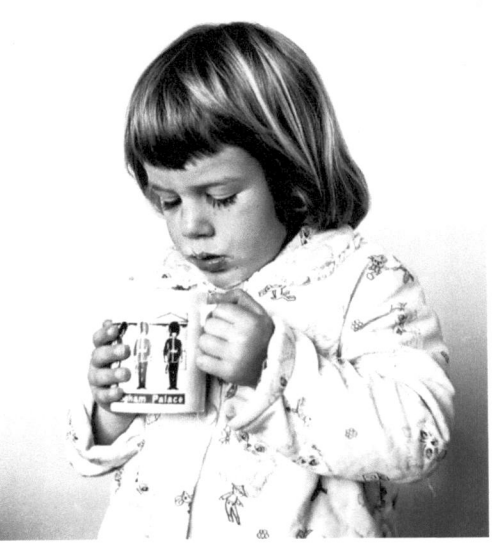

By following his advice I began sending black and white 10x8 prints to a variety of magazines and, to my delight, began making sales. And, while the cheques were nice, I found that the most

1

excitement came from seeing my work in print — something that still gives me a thrill today.

The picture on the previous page is of an early sale of mine to a magazine for early childhood workers in the UK. Sent out on spec as a 10x8 print.

Maybe you are looking for some return on your photography and would like to try freelancing but before you do, be warned; freelancing has never been easy and unless you are the exception to the norm and have photographs that editors are desperate to use and pay you lots of money for, it is hard work, it is frustrating, it is time-consuming, but, if you get a kick out of seeing something that you created in print knowing that an editor is prepared to pay you for using it, then it is addictive.

It is also a business and needs proper records kept to show what images you have sent where and, of course, details of your income and expenditure for tax reasons.

I hope that this book, based on years of experience trying to succeed in this most exciting yet frustrating business, will enable you to experience the thrill of seeing your work in print knowing that somebody thought it worth paying for.

Your Equipment for Freelancing

If you are already producing images that can be reproduced to A4 size then your equipment doesn't need to be changed. However, if your current camera restricts what you can take — some compacts produce good pictures but are not so good when it comes to action because of the delay between the shutter release being pressed and the shutter actually opening — you may like to consider upgrading to a DSLR (Digital Single Lens Reflex) with a minimum of 8 megapixels. This will enable you to make a variety of images with a number of lenses and produce images that will print quite happily up to larger than A3 and be suitable for most uses that they are likely to be put.

I suggest digital as I have found that the benefits far outweigh the disadvantages as far as freelance work is concerned. I no longer have to wait to get my images back from the lab (I recently needed a photo of a plant to accompany an article submission and all I had to do was go into the garden and make the image. Within minutes the picture was on my computer and on to a CD and the submission was ready for the post). I no longer have the expense of film and processing. I do not have to use precious time scanning transparencies — most editors nowadays prefer digital images as they save them time and money in pre-press preparation. I also consider that the results I am getting from my DSLR camera are equal to or even better than I was getting from my film SLR. In fact, at times they are as good as the transparencies I got from my 6x7 camera.

As far as the brand of camera for you to choose, that is a very personal choice. I chose Olympus as I was a fervent OM1 fan. I also liked the fact that they built their digital camera from the ground up and designed lenses specifically for digital. I started with an E300 and have moved to the E510. Neither of these is top of the range but the results from them have been great and perfectly suitable for my business.

If you can afford it, Canon is definitely the professionals' choice especially if your main subject is the landscape. The fact that the top of the range Canons use a sensor the size of the old 35mm film is a big plus factor for the landscape photographer.

When I first moved to a digital camera I thought that my range of

3

filters was obsolete as I was able to vary the white balance for each shot and there was always Photoshop with which to adjust and enhance the image. However, after reading Ross Hoddinott's book, *The Digital Photographer's Guide to Filters* (David and Charles ISBN 978-0-7153-2654-1), and accepting that Photoshop cannot replace what has not been captured, I have dragged out some of my filters and begun using them again.

So what filters are necessary? A polariser is probably the main one — to enable the camera's metering system to operate accurately, make sure that you use a circular polariser and not a linear one. The polariser will reduce reflections and so intensify the colours of, for instance, foliage. It will also darken blue sky and so make white clouds stand out more dramatically.

The other filters that I consider essential for landscape work are the Neutral Density graduated filters. These enable me to reduce the high level of light coming from the sky and balance it with the light coming from the land. These filters are designated by the amount of light reduction that they apply. I have 1, 1.5, 2 and 3 stop filters. I can therefore use two filters to produce most of the variations that I might need.

I also have 1, 2 and 3 stop Neutral Density filters which enable me to slow my shutter speed when I want to blur movement such as when photographing the sea or a waterfall. A recent release has been a 10 stop neutral density filter which really slows things down.

I also have a number of other filters such as warming and cooling filters but I no longer find them as essential as I did when shooting film as I can easily replicate their effects in Photoshop. They generally stay in my old photo bag.

The built-in flash in DSLRs, while not ideal, seems perfectly adequate for most uses especially as it is possible to control the output through the camera's menu.

Other accessories that may be necessary depending upon the type of photography you do are a solid tripod for landscapes, a mini-tripod and a macro lens or a set of close-up lenses for plant and insect photography, and studio lights for indoor portraits. I also use my spotmeter occasionally especially when checking the discrepancy in light between sky and land in landscapes. I could use the facility for spot metering in the camera but I find it easier to use the manual meter which I happen to have left over from my film days. Whether I would invest in one now is debatable.

DSLRs provide a number of ways in which you can save the image that you have just captured. I would recommend most strongly that you use the RAW facility as this does not allow the camera to make judgements that should only be in your province and you therefore end up with an image that has not been 'messed about by a machine' and one that includes as much information as possible which can be brought out in post-processing.

Another item to consider early in the piece is how you handle the images that you have taken. Here's how I do it.

If I am away from my base, I use a laptop to transfer the day's images from the camera's memory card and also burn them to a DVD as a precaution against computer failure. There are other hand-held devices that you can save your images to or you can use a number of memory cards that you process when you get home just as you would have done with film.

When I get back to my base, the images from the shoot are transferred to my main computer into a folder called 'New RAW Images'. I then open up Adobe's DNG Converter (a free download from Adobe at www.adobe.com) and convert the RAW files to DNG and save them in a folder called 'New DNG'. DNG is Adobe's attempt to produce a universal file format that can be read by all computers. At present all camera manufacturers use their own systems — Olympus raw files are ORF.

Having checked them over and discarded the bad ones, I then transfer the DNG files to an external hard drive and, before deleting them from the 'New DNG' folder, I burn them to two DVDs — one as an on-site back-up and the second for storage off-site. Incidentally, when removing the images from the memory card, I re-format the card rather than just deleting the images as I have been warned about the possibility that constant deleting could produce a corrupt card. In fact, I never delete images from the camera while on a shoot, preferring to do so by re-formatting when I have transferred the images I want to my computer.

As I have at present eight external hard drives with images on, I need some form of catalogue to be able to find an image when I need it. I use a Digital Asset Management program called IMatch. It is simple to use and inexpensive compared to some of the more complex programs. IMatch is available from www.photools.com at about $US65 and is discussed in more detail in the next chapter.

Finding Your Pictures

If you've ever tried to find a picture that you know you took but you can't put your hand on it, you will know the benefits of having a system that leads you to it in a trice.

In this digital age there are a number of digital asset management programs (a fancy name for a catalogue) that will do just that. Some are fairly expensive but others are much more affordable and it is one of the latter that I chose and, so far, it has done the job admirably. A search on the internet for 'Digital Asset Management software' will produce a long list of programs that basically will all do the same job with some having more bells and whistles. Two of the favourites are Expression Media (formerly iView MediaPro) and Extensis Portfolio. Neither is cheap.

In the days before digital, I filed my negatives and transparencies in suitable pages that were either put into folders or a filing cabinet. It was a very simple system but it relied upon my memory as to when a picture had been taken to find the image I wanted and that did not always work very well. I then tried a card index system but those systems rely upon being kept up to date and I failed miserably in that area.

As my photography began to concentrate on transparencies, I set up a database in Microsoft Access and, for a while, this worked well but then the administration of it started to lag behind the photography so I failed in that, too.

Then came digital and I didn't have a negative or transparency to file. In fact, I woke early one morning as my sub-conscious battled with the fact that if I had a computer crash I would lose all my digital images — I had recently had a crash that had wiped out a number of my scanned images from transparencies but that was rectified by the simple but tedious task of re-scanning the originals. I was out of bed in a flash and spent hours burning my digital images on to DVDs.

I gave a rundown of my system of saving my images in the last chapter so I will pick up at the point when I have my images on an external hard drive and also backed up on to a DVD. It is now that my budget-priced cataloguing program, IMatch, comes into play. This program indicates when there are new or changed images in the database. One click and the program automatically searches for these additions and saves them to a folder designated by me as 'New Images' ready for me to select the category or categories to which I wish to assign them.

The categories are an essential part of the cataloguing and retrieval system. They are determined and set up by you with the facility to include as many categories and sub-categories as you wish. As more images are assigned to a major folder such as 'New South Wales', I can add a sub-category that will speed up the retrieval of a desired image. For instance, I recently moved to the Snowy Mountains in New South Wales and as I shall obviously be photographing more and more in the local area, I added a sub-category of 'Snowy Mountains' to my 'New South Wales' category. When that sub-category became too large, I added other sub-categories to it such as the four seasons, 'Flora' and 'Fauna' and then when those sub-categories become unwieldy I can add maybe 'Blue flowers' and 'Red flowers' to 'Flora' or 'Natives' and 'Exotics'. The possibilities are endless. Any images assigned to a sub-category will also be shown if you select the main category.

With the new images in the 'New Image' folder, I can assign single or multiple images to a category or categories by selecting them, ticking the necessary categories, removing the tick from the 'New Image' category and pressing 'assign'. You can also apply metadata information such as a caption, copyright details and so on to each image either before assigning them or at any time thereafter simply by clicking on the IPTC button which brings up a form for the image selected.

The images that I file initially are straight DNG images with no adjustments so that I have the image as shot always available. However, those images that have sales potential or those that I have worked on are saved in an unsharpened state as a PSD file (unsharpened because most on-line photo libraries require unsharpened images) in a sub-category file called 'US' (for unsharpened!). This means that when I want to send a picture in that sub-category to a publisher all I have to do is select it from the IMatch catalogue, size it appropriately in Photoshop and sharpen it for the particular publisher. And the system tells me which of my external hard drives the image is stored upon as I point the cursor to the thumbnail. Quick and easy.

As with Photoshop, I only use the facilities in IMatch that I need. There are many possibilities which I may use one day but, at present, I pick and choose and you can do the same. The main attribute is that the program enables me to find images easily. I include scanned transparencies as well as digitally captured images so all my usable pictures are catalogued in one place.

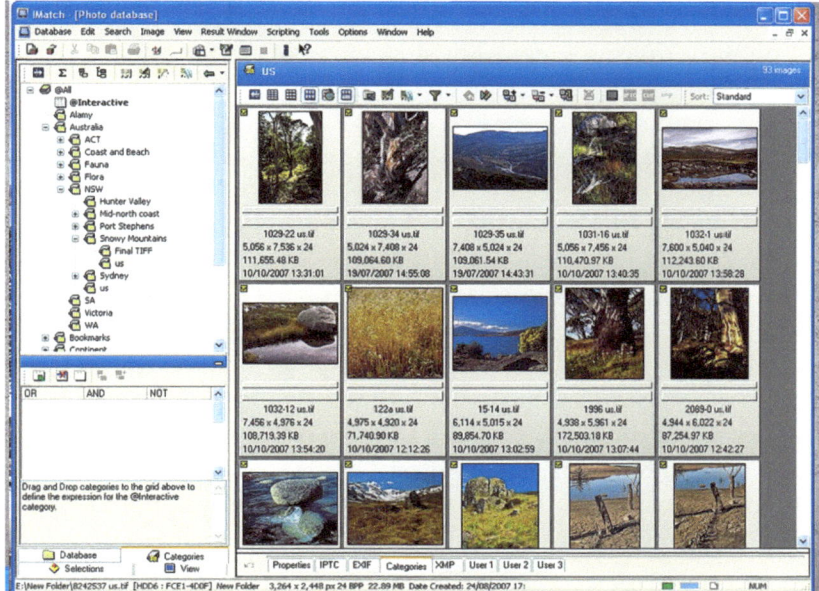

A page from the IMatch catalogue.

Marketing

There are many great photographers who have not succeeded in the freelancing business and many reasonable photographers who have. What's the difference? Their ability to market their product.

It's no good having great photos in your files if they never get to the marketplace.

So, important as websites, scanning, Photoshop, burning to CDs, digital capture, etcetera are, the vital part of a freelance's business is, as it always has been, marketing.

Over a period of time when I have been interviewing a number of successful freelance photographers I have asked how the digital age has affected their working especially since most publications will now accept images as digital files and some even insist on it.

The answers were quite varied indicating that there is still a way to go before consensus is reached about the 'best' way to go about marketing in the digital age.

One of my questions related to websites which we are told from some quarters are vital to any freelance. Two highly successful UK landscape photographers both admitted that their websites would be more successful if they had the time to spend updating them. This was a common theme when talking to many photographers and especially those running a one person business.

Others varied between their websites bringing in small amounts of irregular business and being so successful that they were enlarging that side of the business. Still others saw their website as a portfolio to which they could direct potential clients.

Ross Hoddinott, one of the younger generation of freelance photographers, comments, "I think it's crucial to have an on-line presence. It attracts a limited amount of direct business but it is useful as an on-line portfolio of my work. I often refer potential clients to my site so they can assess the style and quality of my photography."

When questioned about on-line photo libraries the answers were also varied with comments such as, "Sometimes sales come in waves and then it goes quiet for a while" and "As more images are uploaded the sales are increasing. On-line selling is more about quantities. The more images you have on-line, the better your chances of selling."

And, the answers to my question about on-spec submissions were equally varied. But, this time, the answers were basically divided by the experience and reputation of the photographers. The less experienced tended to send material out on-spec with some sending low resolution thumbnails or scans on a CD and others going the high resolution route while the more established did not need to send out on-spec submissions.

So, where does all this leave me and all those freelances working on their own and many with limited time for their business.

First, in answer to the questions I asked above, I do have a website which has brought me some small business for my calendars and e-books. Like Ross Hoddinott, I see my website as a way of having a portfolio that I can direct editors to (I include its URL in my signature on all business e-mails and Ross sends out a well-printed card with all his submissions to publicise his website. The card includes a photo which he changes every other year.). I do have over a thousand of my images with Alamy (www.alamy.com), the on-line library, which has resulted in sales for me to markets I would not have ordinarily reached — Germany, America, Austria for instance.

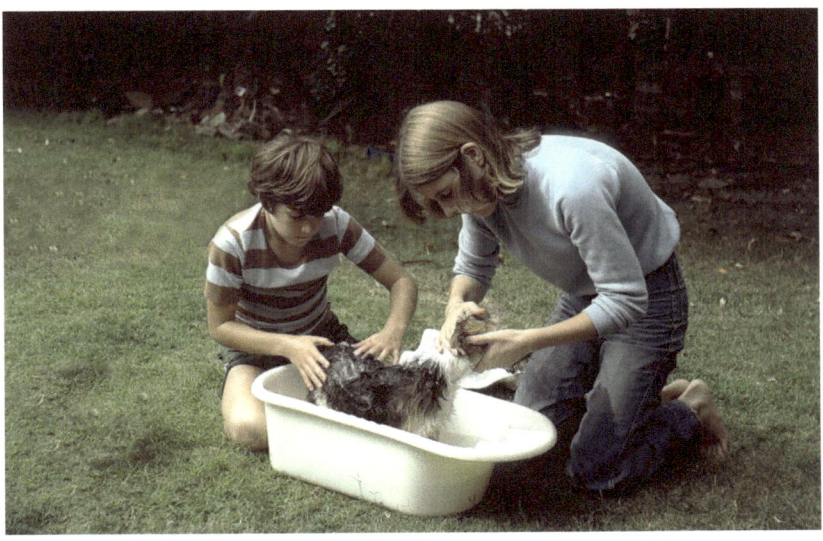

Sold through Alamy to a German publisher

And, yes, I do send out submissions on spec and this is how I do it nowadays.

When I want to send out an image, I open the file in Photoshop, adjust where necessary, reduce to 8 bytes, sharpen and save the result as a 300dpi TIFF file generally to A4 size or larger. When I have the required number for the submission, they are burned to a CD for delivery to the editor.

But, few editors are going to use their precious time to look at a CD when they have no idea what they will see and even if they do have a look, they will not thank you if the files take an age to open.

So, after I have made the high resolution images for a CD, I have a batch action in Photoshop CS4 set to convert the images to 72dpi JPEG files which are burned to the CD in a lo-res folder. Another batch action reduces the size to thumbnails for printing to an index so that the editor can see whether it's worth time to open the CD.

The index is printed on an A4 sheet (I use Epson double-sided matte paper on an Epson 3800 printer) in horizontal mode so that it can be folded to an A5 size after printing. I also choose one image to be used as an A5 cover picture as an indication of quality and, hopefully as a hook to persuade the editor to look at the CD which also has a miniature of the Index Cover image on its label. If all this sounds a lot of effort, do remember that editors are a freelance's potential customers. The alternative to sending high and low resolution images is to just send low res files. The reason I have got into the habit of sending the high res as well is that so many of my submissions go overseas and I'm always hopeful that an editor will use an image he likes if the high resolution file is available immediately. Admittedly, the file could be sent by e-mail (I use a company called High Tail which allows me to send high resolution images by e-mail) or via a website but even these methods require some action on the editor's part and some time to receive them.

Another approach that I am trialling is the use of lightboxes. I can put together a lightbox for an individual editor which only he or she will be able to access via the link that I e-mail to them. I have found that the editors I have approached in this way have generally been appreciative. Of course, this method does require the editor to request the high resolution file of any images of interest but at least the initial contact is quicker than snail mail.

Life changed for the freelance with the advent of the digital age but many things remain the same. If your images are not sharp, well-composed, correctly exposed and interesting then no amount of marketing will sell them. However, if you have all those factors right you stand just as good a chance of making sales as you ever did. It's just the mechanics of marketing that have changed with the advent of digital, in most cases for the better from a freelance's point of view.

But, your pictures need to be in the market place if they are to have a chance of selling.

If you are interested in Microstock (very low prices for royalty-free images that rely on multiple downloads to give you a return on your investment), have a look at two of the biggest, iStockphoto and Shutterstock. You'll find them on the internet.

As a matter of great importance, I do not offer sale of the copyright of my images. What I do offer is Single Reproduction Rights or, in other words, a licence to use the image once. Each extra use, if any, requires an extra payment.

Make Souvenirs with Your Images

Even in the digital age with no film and processing costs, photography is not cheap. When you take into account the cameras, lenses, computers, software, printers, paper, inks and all the upgrades that seem to occur regularly to tempt you to spend more money to get the latest super outfit which will be superseded within months, it appears that it gulps money.

So, how can you recoup some of this outlay? What can you do with all those great pictures that fill your files? They must be worth something.

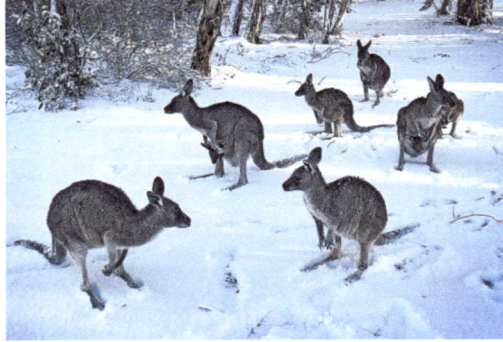

My best-selling postcard — 2000 sold to date

Well, as somebody who over the years has had a go at many projects designed to earn money with my photography let me suggest a way that can produce cash from your camera. Why not use your pictures to produce what I classify generally as souvenir products for your local area? I include in this category such things as postcards, greeting cards, calendars, notecards, bookmarks, and posters.

In this chapter, I shall take each category and explain how I go about making them, the software I use with suggested alternatives, and the materials.

But, first, let me make it quite clear that if you really intend to make some cash from these products, you will have to recognise that you need to treat them as a business project.

You will need to produce professional looking material, you will need to have some method of bringing your product to the attention of possible buyers whether consumers or retailers, you will need to set competitive prices, you will need to keep books of account; in short you will be running a business.

But, perhaps you will prefer to produce items with your photos that you can send or give to your family and friends. At least in this way you are showing your pictures rather than letting them disappear once you have looked at them and moved on to the next image.

Whichever method suits you, why not have a go and give your images some sort of life.

Equipment for Souvenir Production

You will need a computer set-up with a colour printer, a word-processing program, a desk top publishing program, an image processing program, a guillotine or some other method of cutting, and for some of the projects, a laminator and laminating pouches.

For your information, I use an Epson Photo Stylus 3800 printer, Microsoft Word, In Design desk top publishing, Photoshop, an A4 guillotine and an A3 laminator.

You will not need such an advanced printer and can use Open Office which does all that Word does and is free (www.openoffice.org). You can also look for a free desk top publishing program on Google. Instead of Photoshop, you can use Photoshop Elements which is a cut-down version of Photoshop and is therefore much cheaper and an A4 laminator will suffice if you want to make laminated bookmarks.

Bookmarks

Bookmarks are an easy and useful item to start with. I have made mine in a variety of sizes and have settled on a bookmark that is 50x140mm with an image that is 42.5x107.5mm. This enables me to get 8 bookmarks out of an A4 sheet of paper. You, of course,

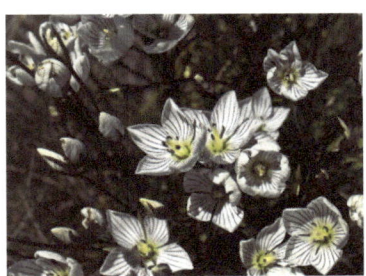

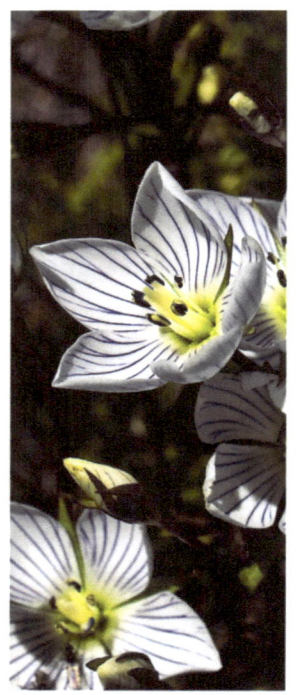

Snowy Bookmark

www.bigwoodpublishing.com
0412 60 30 73

can experiment with sizes to find one that suits you. Bear in mind that your image will have to be cropped to fit into the bookmark.

A vertical image works best but I have, on occasions, used a cropped landscape shape. *(see image on previous page)*

I use either Epson Archival Matt or Ilford Smooth Heavyweight Matt paper and laminate before I cut the individual bookmarks.

Normally, when producing bookmarks to sell into shops, I print on only one side. But, I do offer my bookmarks to businesses as promotional tools and then I print on both sides with the details of the business on the back as the right picture below.

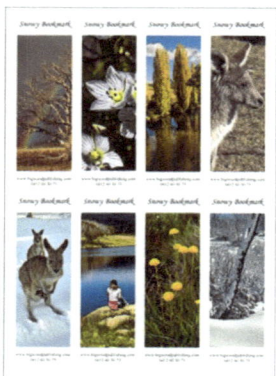

My bookmarks set out on A4 sheets ready for printing and then laminating before being cut up into individual bookmarks.

16

Greeting Cards

Once again, I have produced a number of different sized cards but have settled on a folded size of 175x125mm (a printed size of 175x250mm). This enables a good size image to be displayed. I have also used a number of papers but have finally decided on the Ilford Smooth Pearl as this gives a good finish to the image and is also heavy enough to stand when displayed. I also decided that my cards would be blank inside so that they could be used for any occasion and not have a use by date. However, you can print your own message on the inside for your personal use but I would suggest that if you want to sell them, a blank inside is best.

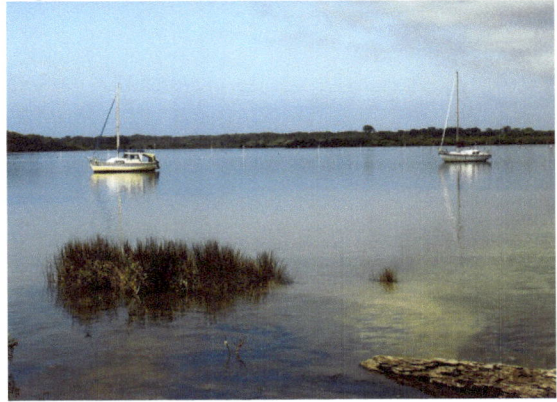

One of my greeting cards

My images fill the front of the card — I make the image 177x127mm so that when I cut them the picture will come right to the edge of the paper — but there is no reason why you cannot put in a border.

I also add the details of the picture on what will be the back of the card which means adding the text upside down.

For retail sale I supply the cards with a 130x180mm envelope sealed in a polypropylene pocket.

Of course, if you do not want to print these cards yourself and prefer to leave the production to a commercial printer, check with him or her first to find out how your material should be presented. The same applies to any of the products in this book.

Notecards

Very similar to the Greeting Cards are what I call Notecards which, as the name suggests are cards that can be used for quick notes such as 'thank you's'.

These are produced in the same manner as the bigger cards except that when I print them myself I use Ilford Archival Matt paper and they are sized to fit 2 cards on an A4 sheet. The cards are 148.5x105mm (printed size 148.5x210mm) with an image that is 137x87mm. This allows a border around the image giving me space to print 'Greetings from the Snowy Mountains' beneath the picture. Details of the image are, once again, on the back of the card and the card is sealed in a polypropylene pocket with a C6 envelope (114x182mm) for retail sale.

Postcards

Postcards are a very popular product for photographers looking to use their own pictures on commercial products. However, postcards are one item that need to be printed by a commercial printer. Mine allows me to print a number of different cards for the total price of the cards ordered plus a small extra charge. In other words, I can order 500 cards of 4 designs for the 2000 card price plus a little extra which is lot cheaper than the 500 card price. I am sure that you will be able to find a similar deal from a printer near you or on the Internet.

I size the image to suit the front of the card and print the details on the back together with the standard layout for a postcard which generally means a space for the message, another for the recipient's address and a rectangle for the postage stamp.

Check with your commercial printer as to what format your postcard should be set out in.

Calendars

I have published an A4 wall calendar for the area in which I live for the last three years. They have sold well through retail outlets plus some sales through my website. My commercial printer provides the date section so all I have to worry about are the images. I try to match the image to the season which seems to go down well. These calendars are prepared in my desk top publishing program and converted to pdf (Portable Document Format) files for sending to the commercial printer. The front cover includes the name of the calendar and those of the photographers while the back has thumbnails of the images included.

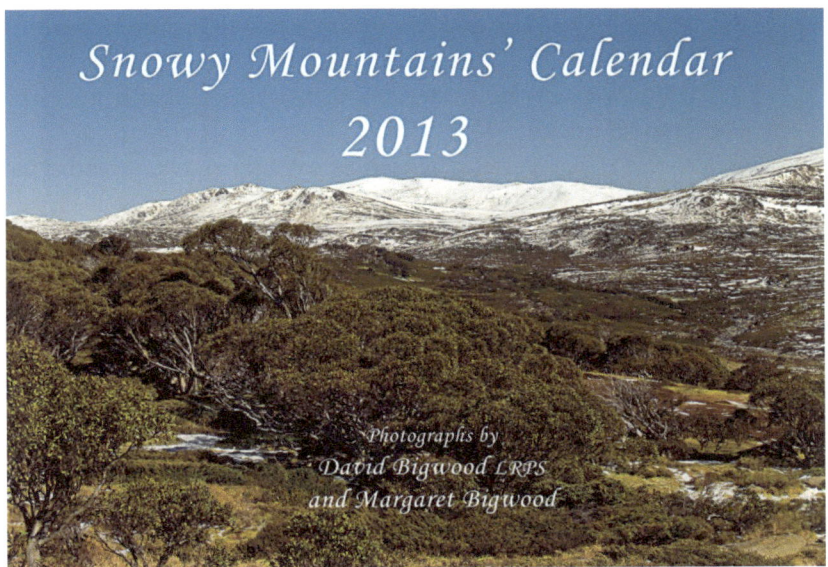

I am now considering producing a higher quality A3 calendar — while the A4 calendar opens up to A3 size, the A3 calendar is printed flat ie with no fold.

I have also produced a desk calendar which fits into a plastic case — like a CD case which I buy from a supplier on-line; search for 'calendar cases' — which opens to provide the calendar stand.

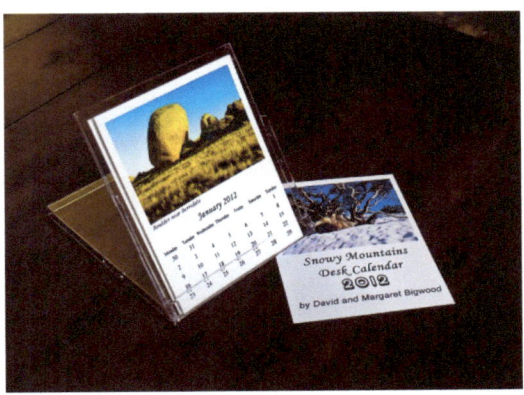

The page size for the desk calendar is 135x105mms with an image size of 95x67.5mms. The page size allows me to print 4 up on an A4 sheet of paper. Once again, these calendars are prepared in my desk top publishing program. I prepare the dates part separately in the program and then copy them to the calendar pages.

For small orders, I print these myself but for larger quantities I go to my commercial printer.

I have offered a larger version which is roughly twice as wide, as promotion pieces for businesses and had some success with it. The larger size allows for promotional material alongside the calendar thus bringing the viewer's attention to the promoting business every day of the year.

There are a number of standard sizes of calendar cases available so choose the size to suit your calendar.

Posters

Another product that makes a suitable item for displaying your photos is a poster. I have toyed with this idea but so far have got no further than mocking up a few possible designs. If I go ahead, I would have these printed by my commercial printer but I am not too sure if the shops I sell to would be prepared to give space to promote them. Some more research is required.

Words and Pictures

Of the hundreds of articles I have had published, only a handful were not illustrated with my pictures. Whether the words sold the pictures or the pictures sold the words is impossible to determine but it seems obvious that a package offered to an editor must make his or her job easier if they do not have to seek pictures to illustrate the words. There is, of course, the proviso that the subject of the article is what they want and the words and pictures are up to scratch.

If you are wanting to make some sort of cash return on the investment you have made in your photography, perhaps you should consider adding words to your pictures.

Getting Started

I appreciate that to some the thought of writing to offer to an editor is mind blowing. Thoughts go back to essays at school, to grammar, to spelling. Aah, it's just too hard!

It needn't be. You don't have to start with long articles as you probably have in your photography files many pictures that can be used as fillers — fillers are short items that editors love when they have a few small spaces in an edition with press time looming; an event that occurs more often than not.

All you have to do to make your picture into a possible filler is to write an extended caption which explains what and where the picture is and add any interesting facts about it. I did this many years ago when I photographed a steam engine that was displayed outside Canberra railway station in the Australian Capital Territory. It turned out that the engine was the first one to haul a train into Canberra which was the reason it was displayed. But, I also found out that the engine had been built in Lancashire in England which gave me the peg to hang the picture and caption on. The picture and fewer than 100 words went off to *Lancashire Life* magazine where it was published and paid for a short time after.

A similar thing happened with a picture I had made of Fort Denison in Sydney Harbour. This time it went to an Australian military magazine where it was published.

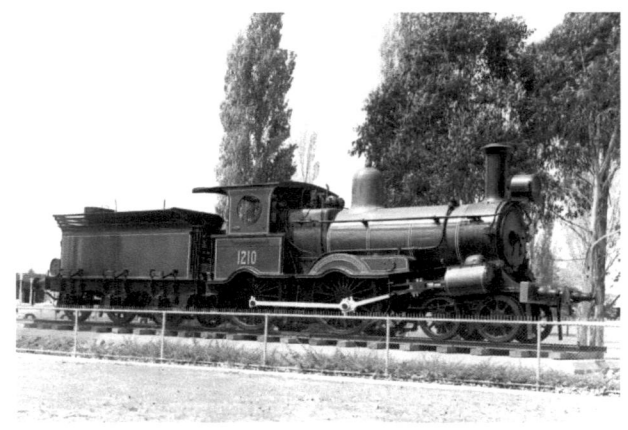

If you need to gain your confidence in writing, these short pieces will help you do it and with the resources of the Internet at your disposal now you will be able to find information that you can use quite quickly. Just do not copy what you find on the web. While there is no copyright in facts, there is in the words used to describe them. So, take the fact and write your own words to explain it.

Practising with these short pieces of writing, especially after you have had a few published and paid for, will gradually encourage you to branch out into your first full articles. But, of course, you may decide to stay with fillers if you are proving that you have the ability to provide what editors want.

Moving On

If you do decide that you want to go the whole hog as it were and have a go at article writing, begin by sorting through your image files and make a note of pictures that could hang together in an article. They may be travel pictures, or items of particular interest to a hobbyist or collector, or pictures that could be used for a 'how to' article. Once you have decided on the pictures and the type of article you will write, start researching the subject and make notes that will help you put together an interesting article.

For example, if you have decided to write an article about a place you have visited recently, look up its history, find out what events have happened there, who of note has connections, how has it changed during its life, what makes it worth visiting. That will give you a start and help you decide whether it is even worth writing about.

If you decide that it is a goer, then, before you start tapping away at your keyboard there is one more thing to do. Decide what publication you are going to send it to. Why? Simply because if it is at all possible, you need to get hold of a copy of the publication you are aiming at so that you can see the type of approach they have in their published articles. You can read the type of language they use, count how many pictures go with an article and how many words are in their articles.

Many magazines do publish contributor guidelines that will explain what they are looking for, what format articles and images should be in and how to submit work. You can find many of these on the internet. They will give you a fair idea of requirements but do try to see the publication as well.

The First Draft

Right, all those decisions made and you have given yourself the green light. Get to your computer, or grab your pen and paper, and start writing. Don't worry about grammar, spelling or any technical things. Just write. Just get down your thoughts, the information you have researched, the feelings you had when you visited the place. Be enthusiastic. You want to give your readers. including the editor you are trying to sell to, a reason to read the whole article and, maybe, buy it or follow in your footsteps.

This first draft of your article needs to be finished without going back to edit anything. Get it down while your mind is white hot. It may be a mess but it gives you something to work on and that is half the battle in writing. Words in your head are all very well but words on paper are invaluable. You can see where changes have to be made and judge how it all sounds. In fact, one of the most effective ways of testing your article is to read it aloud to yourself. You will hear where changes have to be made. Read your writing aloud often. And, 'aloud' is the operative word. That is what I have just done once more with this piece of writing.

So, the first draft is finished. Now you can determine whether you have the information in the most appropriate order, whether there are any glaring grammatical or spelling mistakes, whether explanations are clear, whether the article does what you want it to do. The first draft is, of course, just that. The first. I often find that articles end up in second or third drafts or even more before they are ready to go out into the world.

And now, you can consider the polishing of your writing. If you are not confident in your use of grammar, find someone who is and get them to edit your work. Bear in mind that this may cost you money so if you plan to go on writing I suggest that you find a book that will help you get your grammar correct.

Presentation

Once your article has been edited by you or someone else then it is time to get it ready to go to your selected market. This is how I do it. I print a hard copy on A4 size paper using Times New Roman font in size 12 with double spacing between lines. I start with the title centred about a third of the way down the first page with my name below it. I then leave a line before starting the text of the article. I try to avoid having a paragraph run over onto the next page but that is not necessary, just something I like to do. At the top of this first page, on the left hand side I type the rights I am offering — for Australia, I type "First Australian Serial Rights" assuming it is the first time the article has been offered in Australia. The 'serial' does not imply that it is part of a series but that it is being offered to a publication that is published regularly like a magazine as opposed to a book. Opposite this on the right hand side, I type the number of words in the article.

I also arrange for each page to be numbered (Microsoft Word can take care of this automatically for you). On the last page, I type my name and address at the bottom.

A cover page can be added with a repeat of the rights offered and the word count at the top, the title half way down and your name and address at the bottom.

I then burn the text of the article with single space between lines to a CD along with the images I am offering (a few more than I think they will use) as uncompressed 300dpi TIFF files to close to A4 size. I also burn the same images to a folder as low resolution (72dpi) JPEG files. This is so that an editor can quickly look at the pictures without waiting for the high resolution files to open. These are there for when the decision has been made to use your article. I also provide a printed index of thumbnails so that the editor can easily see what you are offering without having to load the CD into their computer.

The index is printed on an A4 sheet (I use Epson double-sided matte paper on an Epson 3800 printer) in horizontal mode so that it can be folded to an A5 size after printing. I also choose one image to be used as an A5 cover picture as an indication of quality and, hopefully as a hook to persuade the editor to look at the CD which also has a miniature of the Index Cover image on its label.

The Index also indicates the rights I am offering for the text and that for the images I am offering Single Reproduction Rights.

This may seem a lot of work but do remember, as I have written before, you are trying to sell your work to the editor and he or she is the customer. Anything we can do to make it easy for the editor to say, "I'll buy it" is to our benefit.

All of the above assumes that you will be mailing your article. To date, I have found that most of the magazines I have dealt with still want material delivered the traditional way but this is changing slowly.

If your publication accepts submissions by e-mail, it will probably set out exactly how it wants it sent and you will have to follow those instructions.

Finding Your Markets

Finding markets for your words and pictures is sometimes a frustrating business. Obviously, if you are a regular reader of a magazine you will have a head start as you will be familiar with the type of article it uses. Your newsagent is another source of information but, don't just browse and read for free after all he or she is in business so buy the magazines that interest you. Or, go to a library.

There are a number of books that are published each year for the benefit of writers. In the UK it is the *Writers' and Artists' Yearbook*, in America it is *The Writer's Market*, in Australia the *Australian Writer's Marketplace* and, of particular interest to photographers in the UK, *The Freelance Photographer's Market Handbook*. Other countries will have their own publications and there is, of course, the internet.

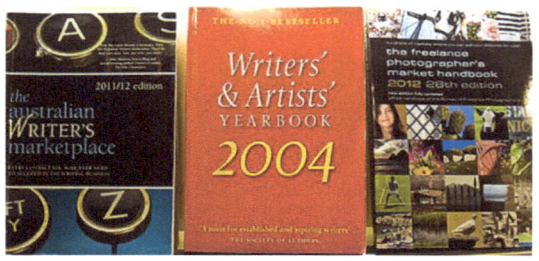

As far as topics are concerned that are suitable for illustrated articles, those that spring instantly to mind are travel, photography, how to, history, profiles of individuals who have done interesting things and collections. No doubt, you will be able to think of more.

Don't forget that in this digital age there are magazines that only appear on the internet and some do pay for articles.

Words and pictures do go together and freelancing as a writer and photographer can be a profitable business as well as allowing your images to be appreciated by people who would otherwise never see them.

Examples of some Images that have Sold

The following images show you some of the images of mine that have been published in a wide variety of magazines, calendars, books, showcards, postcards, and in some places that I have no knowledge of except that a library has paid me when it has made a sale of one of my pictures that they have on file.

The aim is to show you the variety of images that can be used and how some very ordinary subjects can appear in print if the image does the job for the publisher.

You will note that a number of pictures are shown as having been used with articles I have written so this is an opportune moment to remind you that while pictures are said to be worth a thousand words, sometimes it is the words that enable a picture to be published. Even if you do not feel competent enough to write a full blown article, remember that editors are often pleased to have a picture with an extended caption to fill some of the awkward spots that always seem to end up in a layout.

As a final comment, no matter how good your images are, if they don't get out into the market place they will have no chance of appearing in print. While rejections are not pleasant, they are a part of this freelancing game which even the most well known photographer will receive. So, don't let them discourage you because, as all successful freelances have learned, perseverance pays.

The Pictures

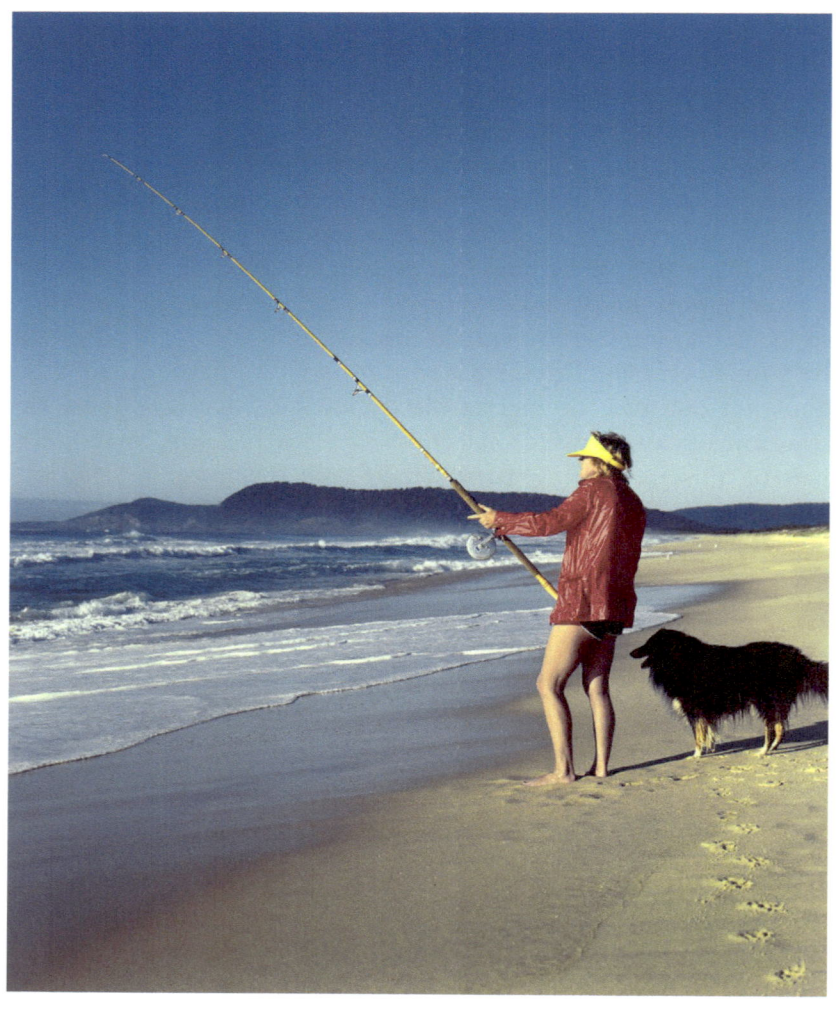

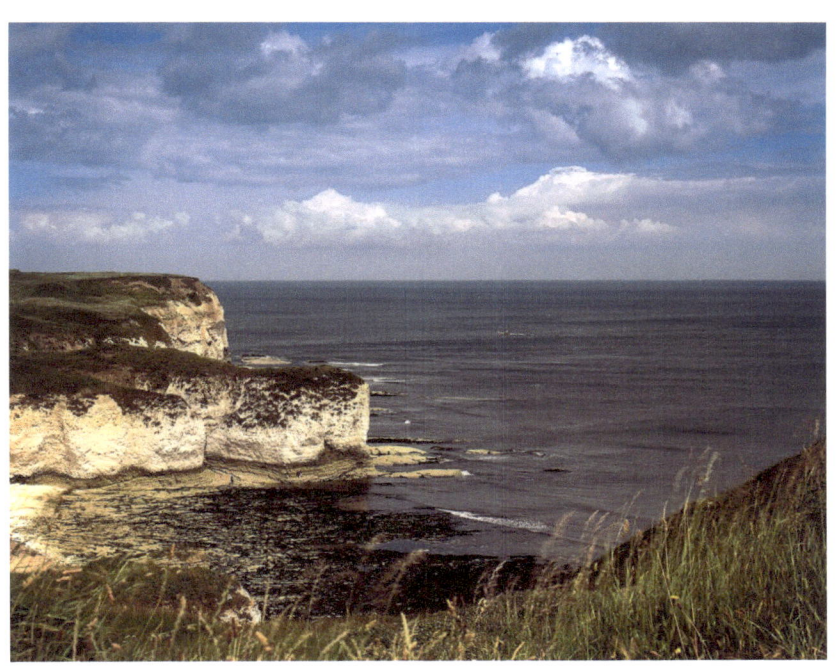

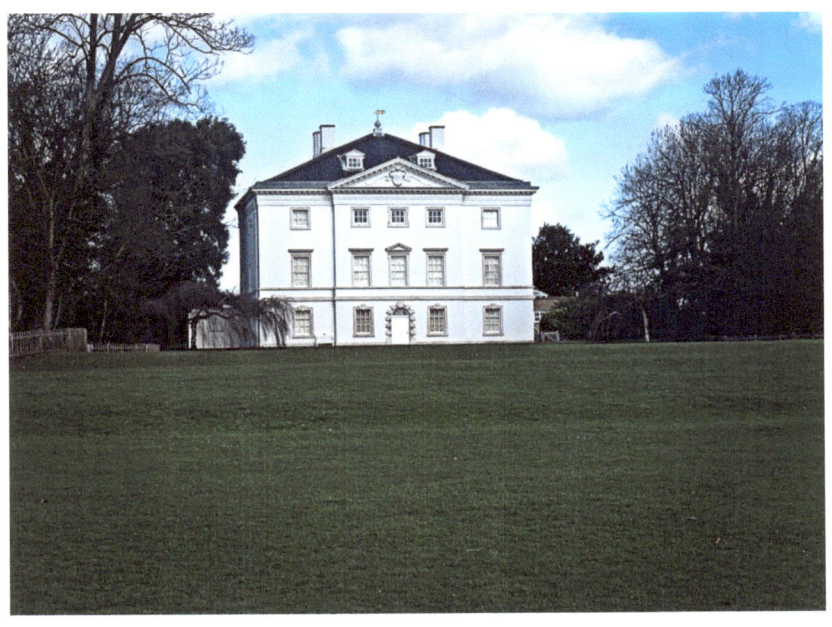

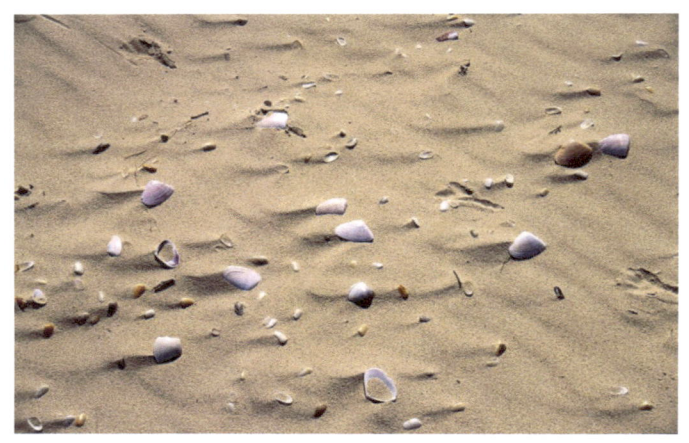

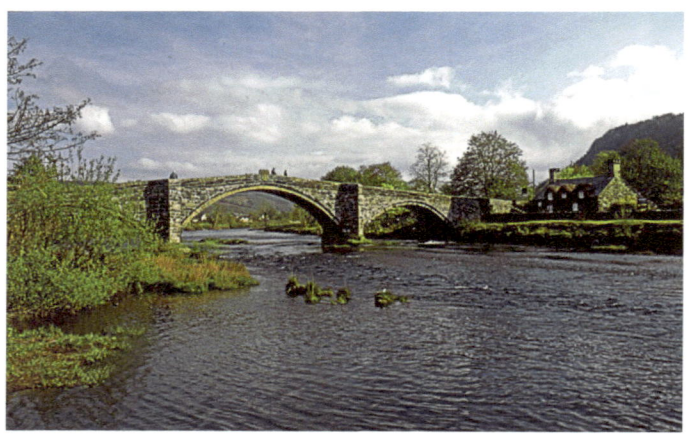

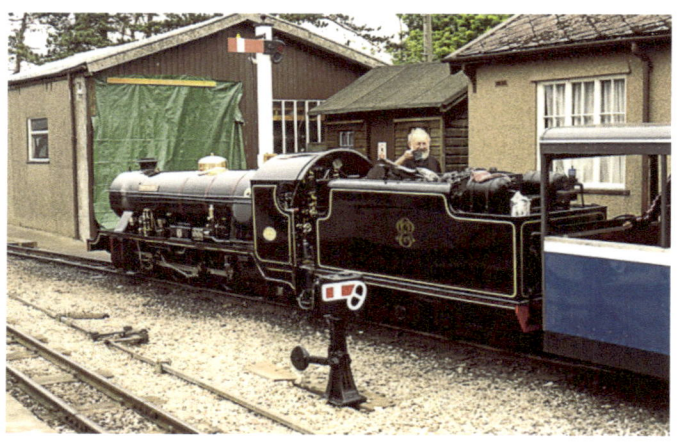

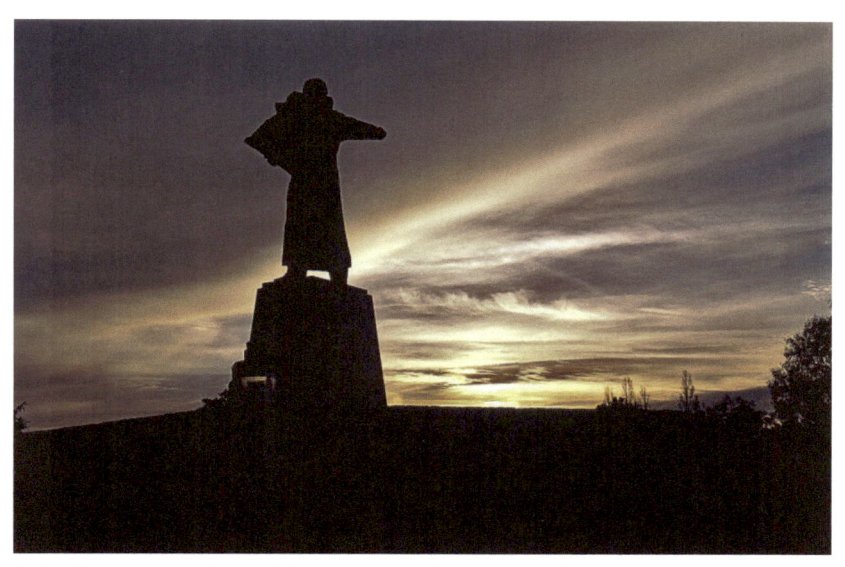

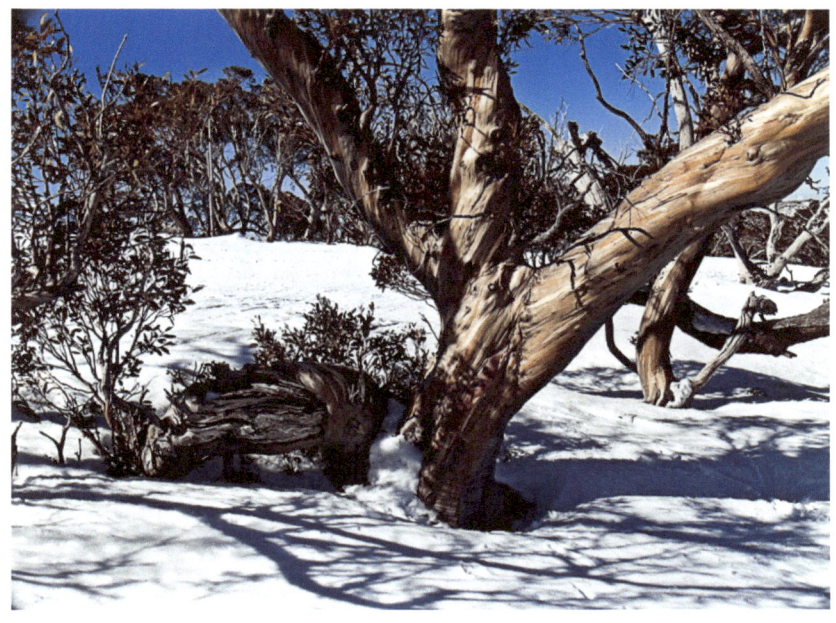

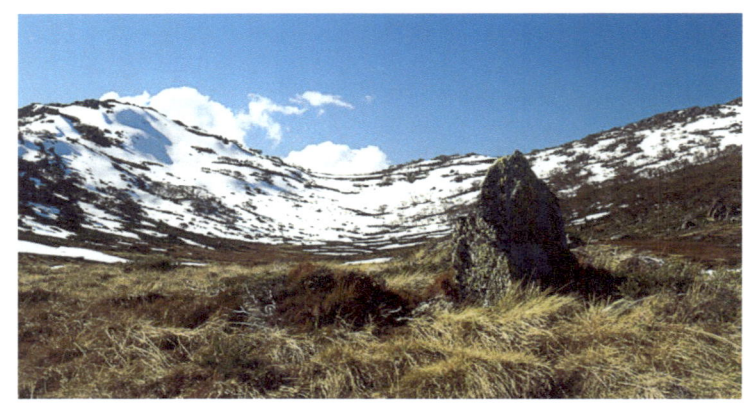

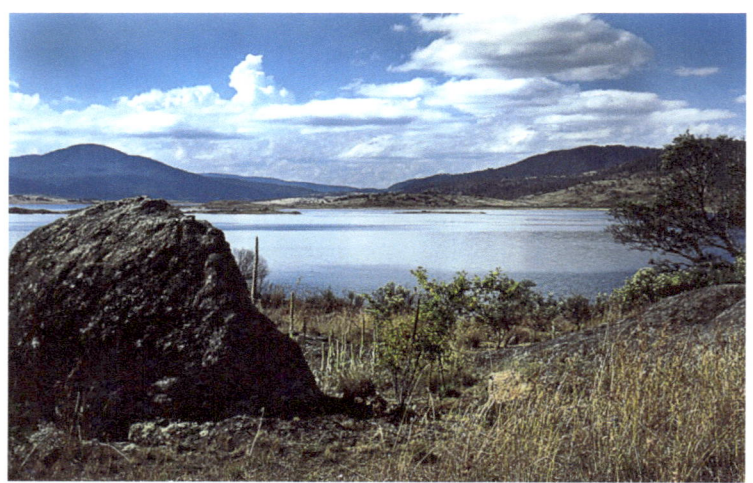

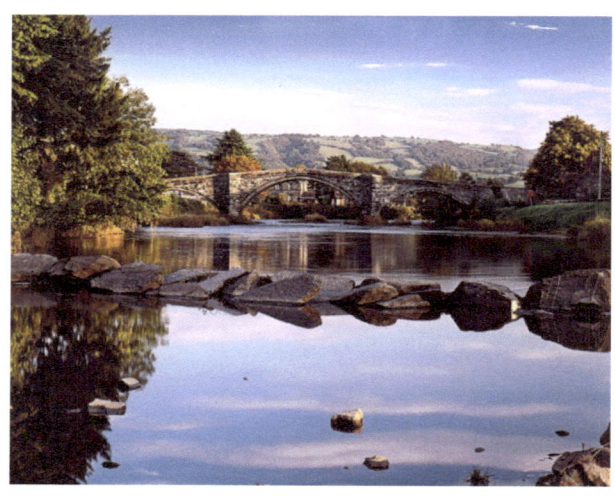

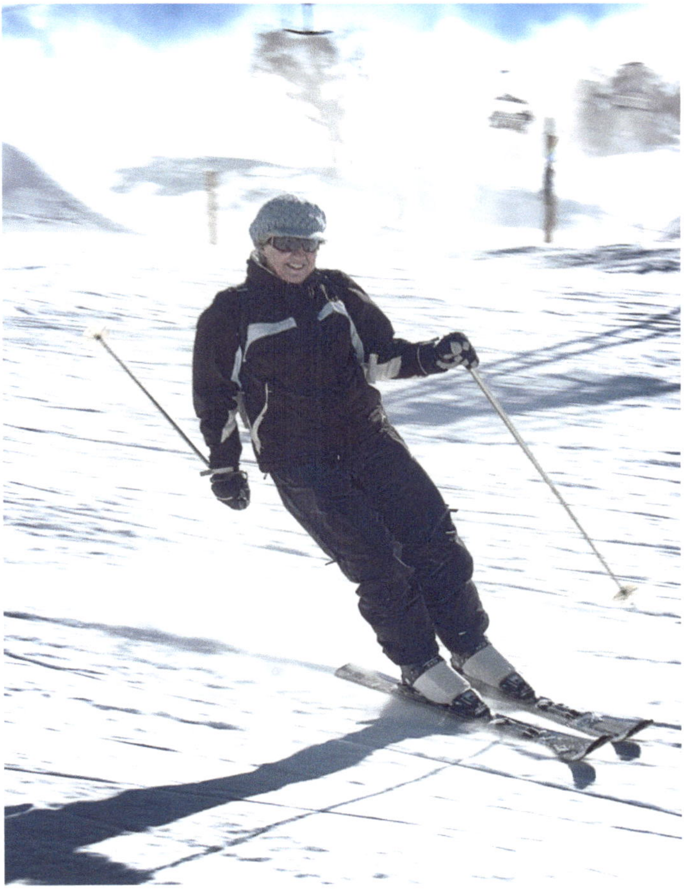

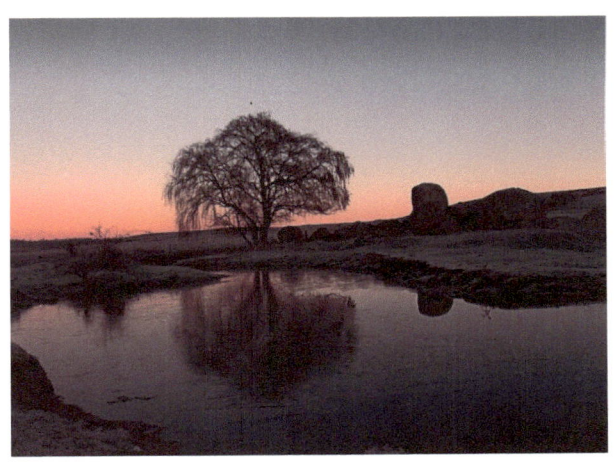

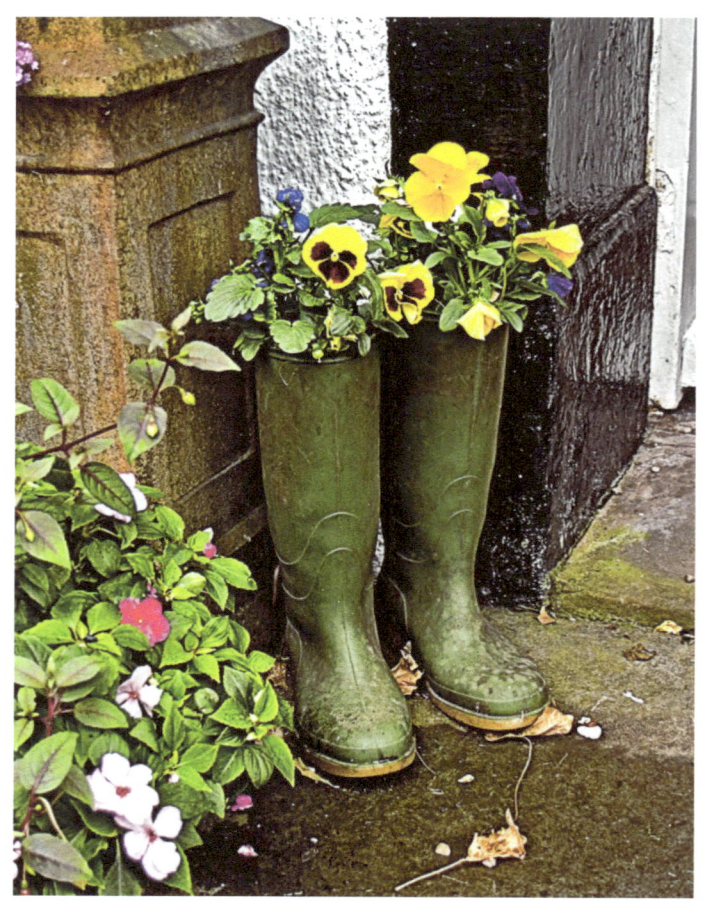

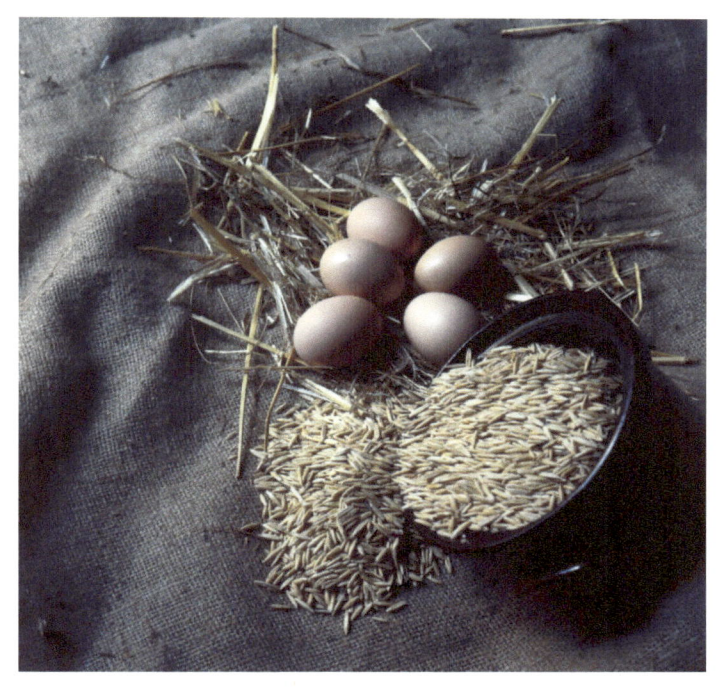

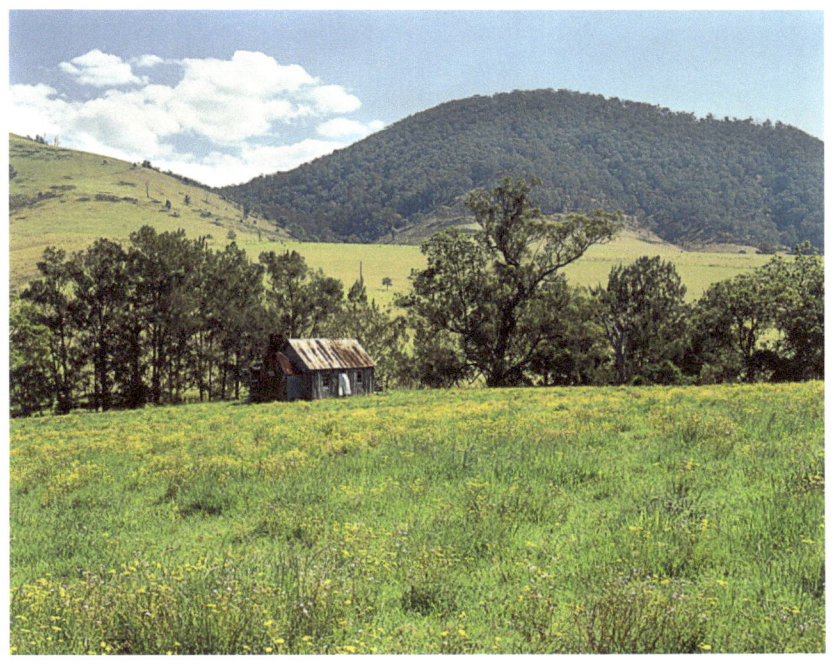

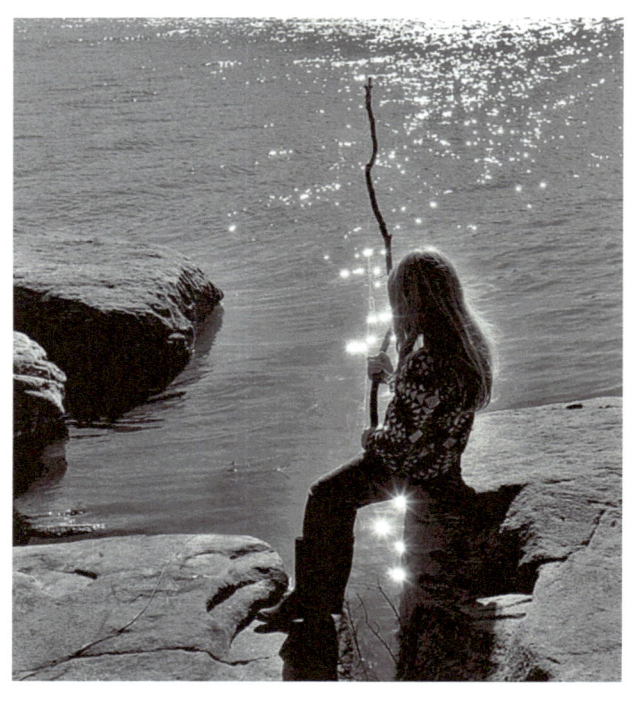

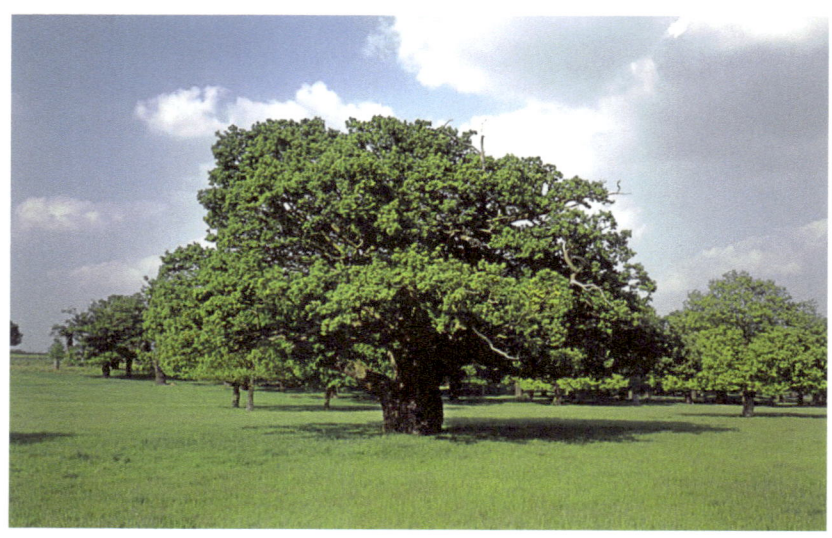

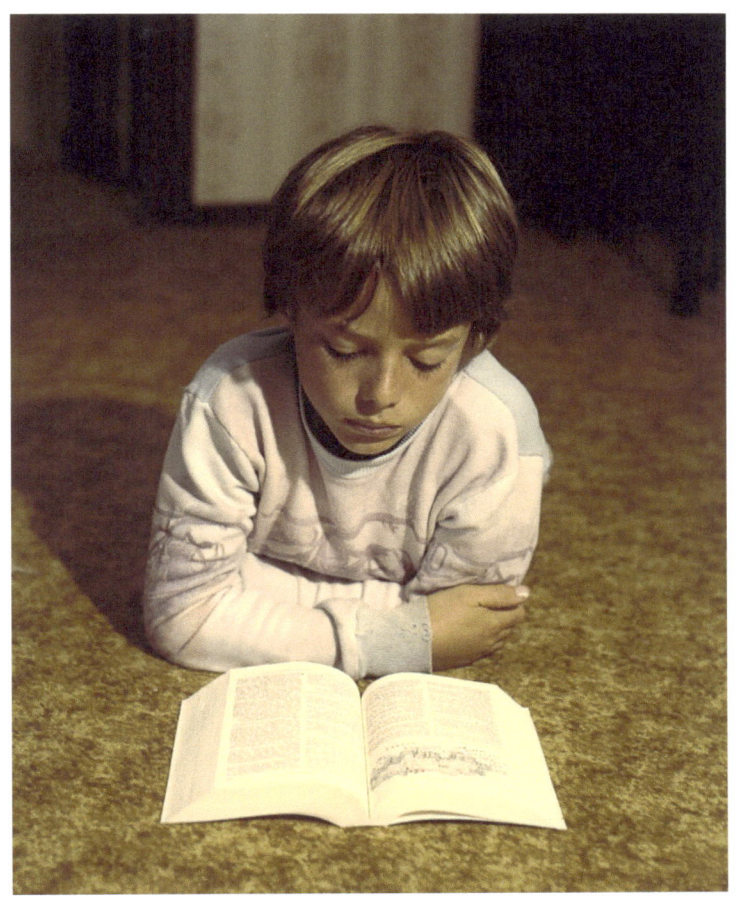

If you want to see the details of these pictures plus more images, please see my e-book, *Images that Sell* at Smashwords (http://tinyurl.com/ofbqeeg) or through Amazon (http://tinyurl.com/pb2aw7y)

Rejections

It is a nasty word with all its implications of 'failure'. But, it is a word that we as freelances have to get used to and accept it for what it really is, an indication of one editor's opinion which could stem from a number of factors. He or she may not like the picture (which is their right); they may have another (in their minds) better picture of the same subject; they may have covered that subject recently; the picture doesn't fit in with the magazine's mission, and so on and so on. I am assuming, of course, that the picture is correctly exposed, clean, well composed and sharp.

So what do we do when images are rejected or should I say, 'not accepted on this occasion'?

What I do is to look carefully at them to make sure that there are no blemishes that I should have picked up and, assuming all is in order, I send them back out into the wide world to the next editor on my list. That way, I have no time to sit and fret about my 'failure'.

Questions can be e-mailed to info@bigwoodpublishing.com